Discover the perfect Managing Director of your business... YOU!

39 steps forward and 39 reasons why and how
you will lead your own small business to success.

By Richard Walters

Management Pocketbooks Ltd.,
14 East Street, Alresford, Hampshire SO24 9EE
Tel: +44 (0)1962 735573 Fax: +44 (0)1962 733637
E-mail: pocketbks@aol.com Web: www.pocketbook.co.uk

First published 2000
©2000 Richard Walters
Designed by Steve Tully

The right of Richard Walters to be identified as the author of this work has been asserted in accordance with the Copyright Designs and Patents Act 1988.

A catalogue record of this book is available from the British Library
ISBN no.1 870471 83 0

Printed by Ashford Colour Press, Gosport, Hants

To all business owners

for taking risks

INTRODUCTION
One of my favourite lines from the Strategic Planning Toolkit is "Everything is easy, if you know how to do it".

I was never very good at science when at school. I would imagine that if I spent a lifetime doing nothing else, and I mean nothing else, but studying how to be a chemist eventually I could claim to be a reasonable chemist. If this is true, and we can develop expertise with sufficient time and attention given, then why not speed up the whole process by learning from others' experience? You don't have to learn the hard way. Running a small business is not a new or unique experience.

Many, many others have done this. They have made mistakes, learned, succeeded, gone bankrupt or just made a living. I believe there are some basic business truths that consistently crop up in all quality management books and more importantly are learned through experience. I have chosen 39 of those which I believe are the most important and recurring truths. These are my personal choices. There are many others. Some may be familiar to you, others will be new, but hopefully all will speed up your process of learning and help you create success for you, the people who work with you and your family. Good luck and enjoy the journey.

Richard Walters

ABOUT THIS BOOK

The book is set out in an orderly form.

It has to be. If you have ever studied any of the great artists of history, you will find their creative and flowing works of art were meticulously planned and designed, in a totally orderly fashion to create incredibly beautiful and innovative perspectives.

I am not claiming to be a great artist but without discipline creativity is just a concept.

If it worked for Leonardo da Vinci why not try it yourself?

The steps are numbered 1 to 39 .

THE WHY OF THE STEPS

Why is this so? Why this step will move you forward in your journey of success in business.

THE HOW OF THE STEPS

What actions to take for success.

The actions are guides for further specific detailed steps you will take on an ongoing and continuous process. Some steps will hit a chord with you, others may not. Those that are appropriate will change from time to time depending upon where you are in your life.

You will be surprised to find how one small concept can be inspirational to you. My suggestion is that once you have read the book you keep it with you at work for a quick read if you are in planning mode, feel in a rut or things just aren't working out. *Let's start the ascent!*

BELIEFS AND WISDOM

"Our mind determines our attitude. You cannot always control circumstances, but you can control your own thoughts"

Charles E Popplestone

SECTION 1
Beliefs and Wisdom

Steps

SECTION 1 – BELIEFS AND WISDOM

STEP 1
You are the perfect MD of your business

WHY

You understand the business. You are passionate and you are totally committed to it. There seems to be a tendency for business owners to underestimate their ability to manage their own businesses. It probably comes from their origins as technicians or sales people. The truth is **no one, literally no one** is better qualified to lead your business than you. *Trust me; there are very few exceptions.*

HOW

Believe you are the perfect leader.

You can and will do it. It is as simple as that.

Don't let anyone tell you any different.

STEP 2
Your business is the mirror image of you

WHY

This one is a bit scary! If you think about this carefully, it actually gives you a great chance to create the business **you** want. How often has your business performance seemed to mirror how you yourself feel at the time? All you have to do is look at **yourself.** Now there's a challenge!

HOW

Literally just recognise it. Don't beat yourself up. *It's good, not bad news.*

STEP 3
Success has many
measures. The only
one that really matters
is your own

WHY

It doesn't matter what anyone says to you. You are the only one that matters on this measure of success. It will **always** be this way. To understand what you have to achieve to be successful, you **must** know your own measure of success.

HOW

Identify your measures of success. Develop these into your goals. Target them and write them down. *Then you know what success is.*

STEP 4
You must have
a purpose

WHY

Just making money is not enough. Your business is the route to fulfilment. When you start in business it may seem that the main objective is to 'make piles of money'. Believe me this is not so. It is certainly not enough to sustain you through your business working life. You probably will, or already have, become unemployable after tasting the independence and freedom of owning your own business. Therefore, you are in it for the long haul. You must have fulfilment to sustain your efforts. I'm afraid this all points to needing a higher purpose.

HOW

Take time out from the day to day running of the business to think about your reasons for being in business. *What gives you the buzz? Write them down! This is your purpose.*

WHY

Visualise your future to the n'th degree. We all know great sports people do this. They visualise their success right down to the smallest detail.

Why would we avoid doing this with our business? It doesn't guarantee success, but you can guarantee you will not have success if you **don't even know what it looks like!**

HOW

Regularly visualise in daydreams your future successful business. Make it feel real. Communicate your vision to others. See it so vividly it is crystal clear in your mind what this looks like. This may appear a bit 'off the wall' but if it works for Olympic gold medallists, why not try it yourself?

STEP 6
Success is belief,
added to vision
followed by action

WHY

What your parents probably taught you is wrong. **Hard work never made anyone wealthy!** If you have belief in yourself and you have the vision to identify your goals you have the major component parts of success. But then the critical point. Without action, consistent and focused, you will not achieve success. Real wealth can only be achieved by leverage of others' time, mass selling of designs or business inventions or processes.

All the great franchises are this.

HOW

Stand back from your business and identify leverage opportunities.
Simply growing your business based upon systems and processes is sufficient, but before doing this be sure the model works!

If you love what you do,
you increase your chances
of success dramatically

WHY

One possible route to great success is luck. But this is not a factor to be relied upon! Another is meanness and Scrooge-like tendencies. In my experience this works, but is not to be recommended as it brings with it a **miserable life.** The route to success is to love what you do. This makes it easy to be passionate (which is essential) and sees you through those inevitable dark days.

HOW

Recognise that you love your work and business.
If you don't, change your role, or more drastically, change your business!

Noel Coward said *"Work is more fun than fun".*

WHY

The great Earl Nightingale said "If you are looking in the pot of reward, you are looking in the wrong place. You should be looking in the pot of service".

Give great service and you will be rewarded with loyal customers. **This is a basic law of business.** Fight this rule at your peril. If you become a 'business taker', you may not be in business for too long.

HOW

Believe it. Give great service. *That simple.*

STEP 9
You cannot manage time, only how you use it

WHY

Prioritising your actions is critical. A lot of hogwash is talked about stress and time management. Why manage something you don't want? Busy is a four-letter word. It is a 'can't do' word. **What** you do is so much more important than **how much** you do.

HOW

Use daily planning sheets to prioritise your actions. Grade actions and check them off when performed. Have a clear desk for a clear mind.

You literally can only do one thing at a time. It is torture to clutter your mind with physical mess.

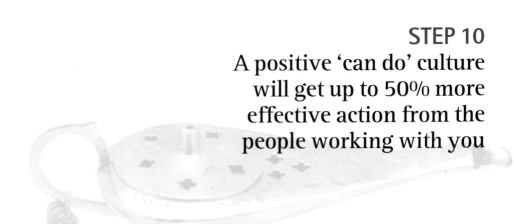

STEP 10
A positive 'can do' culture will get up to 50% more effective action from the people working with you

WHY

People are not machines. They are minds with bodies, not bodies with minds. If your people feel they can solve problems and positive thinking is the accepted norm, they will achieve great things. Positive thinking does not mean unrealistic optimism. People's attitude is so important. You can teach skills to people with the right attitude. Just try teaching attitude to skilled people!

HOW

Negative thinking and acting should be discouraged at all times. Talk positive. Write positive. Acknowledge your positive business culture to all you work with. *Shout it from the rooftops*. Negativity spreads like wildfire. It is contagious. Make champions of your positive thinking people. If you are positive, you already have a competitive edge.

PLANNING

*"I see that my steadfast desire was alone responsible
for whatever progress of mastery I have made.
The reality is always there, and is preceded by vision,
and if one keeps looking steadily the vision
crystallises into fact or deed"*

Henry Miller

SECTION 2
Planning

Steps

STEP 11
You have and live
one life

WHY

Your business life and your home life are not separated. When you have an argument with your husband/wife/life partner, you don't totally escape the emotional consequences as soon as you walk into the office or factory. Equally, when you are worried about the business and wake up at 4.00 am you are usually at home! One life, not two people. (Incidentally, does anyone know why it's always 4 o'clock?)

The key to happiness when you own your own business, as in life, is **balance**. As a business owner, your business is a vital part of your life, but not all of it.

HOW

Make your business work for you. Design it and strategically plan to make it give you **more** from life not less. Whatever you do, ensure it is new, challenging and enjoyable. Understand that your business is a gift. *Plan for your whole life as one plan.*

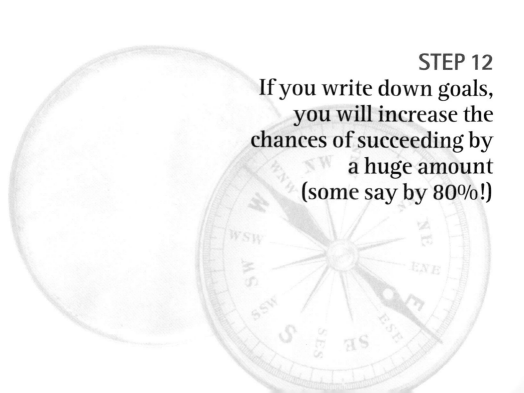

STEP 12
If you write down goals,
you will increase the
chances of succeeding by
a huge amount
(some say by 80%!)

WHY

If you don't know where you are going .... you will probably get there.
Clearly defined goals are critical to success, particularly in business.
Writing these goals seems to bring them into the present and thus on the
path to achievement.

If you plan for what you have, you will get more of the same.
Don't do this please.

HOW

Take at least one day out of a year with a trusted facilitator to identify and write
down your goals. Create your own Strategic Plan. *Write out these goals daily.*
It really does make a difference.

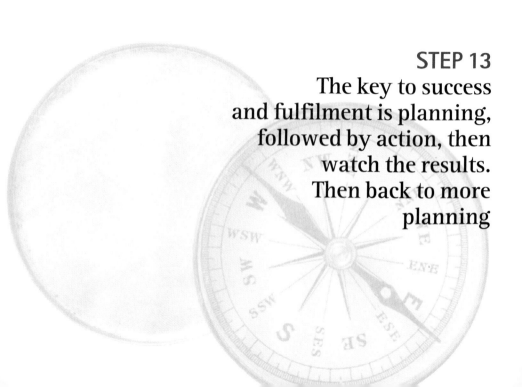

STEP 13
The key to success
and fulfilment is planning,
followed by action, then
watch the results.
Then back to more
planning

WHY

This one is important. If you want to feel in control, you must plan then act upon your plans. Results will follow. Review these results and plan again. You do not want to feel that you are drifting out of control.

HOW

Be disciplined. Use strategic planning techniques to plan for success.

STEP 14
Selling your business is the least likely exit route for you

WHY

Many of us started in business with ultimately selling our business as the main aim.

Statistically it is unlikely you will sell your business. Some people buck the statistics in spite of the fact that to sell a business at a good price a number of factors must be in place. Let's list them. Long term market opportunities. Sound and structured management. Profitability. Growth prospects. Little reliance upon you. Although 9 out of 10 of all statistics are inaccurate, I think you get my point. **It's tough to get all this right.**

HOW

If you are set on selling your business, plan for it and make it completely self-sufficient over a period of years. Look at other exit routes as alternatives. Consider the real financial alternatives. Taking bonuses from a successful business over many years can create great personal wealth. This is a form of exit, a*nd is probably the exit route that will give you the most control.*

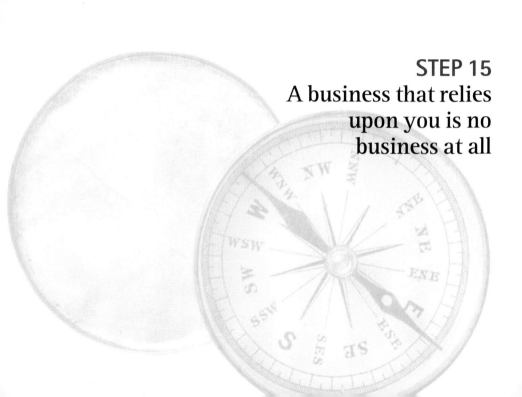

STEP 15
A business that relies upon you is no business at all

WHY

If you are the pivotal point of your business, that business becomes sensitive and unstable. Look upon yourself as filling a number of roles, not the other way around. In other words, do you create the roles to fit you? If so, you set yourself up for stress, pressure and failure.

Remember leverage covered in Step 6?

HOW

Give yourself a job description. Analyse your job into areas of work. Plan to make changes to facilitate your promotion to 'Non-Executive Chairman'.
It's the only career you are ever going to have. *Plan to get to the top!*

STEP 16
Never let the tax tail wag the dog!

WHY

Although taxation is unpleasant, you will go down blind alleys if you let strategy be dictated by tax saving. This is a trap fallen into by many business owners. Balance in planning is vital for success. Letting tax planning dictate is not balance.

HOW

Have a strategy and then follow and implement this with a tax strategy, not the other way around.

EASY TO FORGET BUT OBVIOUS

"I never deny; I never contradict; I sometimes forget"

Benjamin Disraeli

Steps

SECTION 3 – EASY TO FORGET BUT OBVIOUS

WHY

Pots of gold don't exist. Success **really** is a journey, not a destination.
Many people delude themselves into believing that 'The Big One is on its Way'.
Don't chase illusions. Create your own reality.

HOW

Very simple. Strategically plan for what you want. *You have probably worked out that I am passionate about strategic planning. Why? Because it works.*

STEP 18
Every business is
fundamentally a
bunch of people

WHY

It's just that, the people who work for you, your customers and your suppliers. This is a point which is so totally obvious and yet so often missed. All these groups of people constitute your business. **Don't ever forget this, and remember that between these groups communication is vital.**

HOW

Value yourself, your staff, your customers and even your suppliers. Communicate this to all concerned. *The rewards will be enormous.*

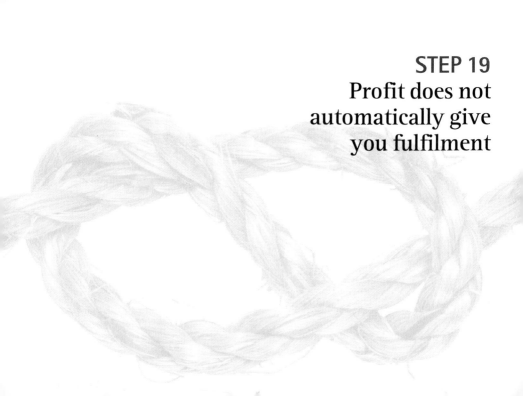

STEP 19
Profit does not automatically give you fulfilment

WHY

We all know this is true, but most of us don't want to believe it. It's a bitter disappointment, isn't it? We know financial independence is so important and yet profit does not automatically give you fulfilment. What a conundrum. It is almost heresy for an accountant to admit this, but it's true!

The truth is that financial independence gives choice. The freedom of choice that follows gives you fulfilment.

HOW

Always look at costs as investments in building your business. If they are not justifiable investments, don't make them. Aim for freedom, not profit. They may be the same, they may not.

WHY

I don't know why, it just seems to be so. Perhaps it's those statistics again! It could be a law of nature. But don't worry, when it happens hold your nerve, and know that when you get through the rough patch you will be even stronger and wiser.

HOW

Keep strategically planning. Hold your nerve with confidence. This doesn't guarantee success but you will guarantee failure if you don't.

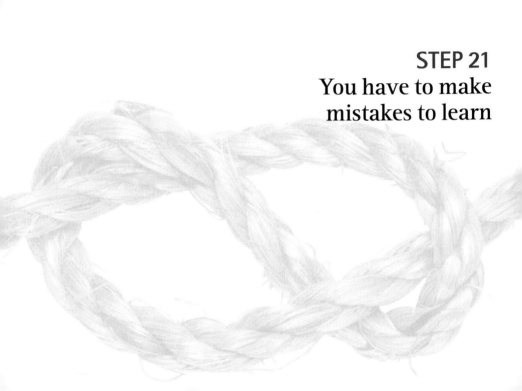

STEP 21
You have to make
mistakes to learn

WHY

It's tough, this one, but true. True in life, true in business. Some people never learn! Successful businesses do. Business is about risk and reward. **How can you aim for high reward if you don't risk mistakes?**

HOW

Encourage a culture of 'opportunities to learn' for everyone in your business. Don't blame. There is a phrase **never ever** to use for mistakes made, and that is C – – K U P !

STEP 22
Create a 'shift up for challenge' culture

WHY

If you want to keep moving forward, this is a must. If you don't move forward, your business will stagnate. The old adage is true 'If you stand still in business, you go backwards'.

A 'shift up for challenge' culture means everyone from you to the most junior team member is committed to learning new skills and 'shifting up' to make room for others below. This approach encourages the right change culture for the modern business world.

HOW

Let your team know that this is the culture. Write it down. Buy them into it. Live it yourself, consistently and with passion.

STEP 23
Your business is a sales and marketing business

WHY

I expect you said to yourself 'No it's not, I'm a graphic designer', 'No it's not, we are engineers', or whatever you trade in.

Every business is a sales and marketing business, selling a particular range of products or services. However, this does not mean quality products, timeliness, price etc do not matter. They do.

But without sales and marketing in whatever form, you have no business at all.

HOW

Give sales and marketing its rightful prime place in planning. Invest all you can in this area as part of a strategic sales plan. Respect the professional skills needed to sell.

STEP 24
The art of
communication
is listening

WHY

Very few of us really listen. How often are you thinking of your reply before the person talking to you has finished speaking? If you learn to listen you will discover things you once missed. You will also be more respected by others.

HOW

Resolve to listen more. Work at this and practice. Notice the benefits. Perhaps even write them down.

This will powerfully repay your efforts.

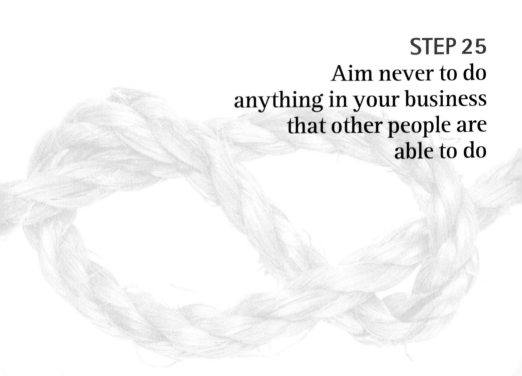

STEP 25
Aim never to do
anything in your business
that other people are
able to do

WHY

Another tough challenge. Because this is often how we justify our existence. If you don't you are not shifting up. It's a good rule to keep you on your toes. Do you want to be the reason your business stagnates? Of course not.

HOW

Every so often ask the question of yourself 'Am I doing only those things that only I can do?'. Answer honestly. You may not be able to change things at that moment but plan to do so as soon as possible.

Tigerish perseverance is a critical ingredient of business success

WHY

Stay around long enough doing the right thing and you will be successful.
You do need stamina to be successful in business. Strength of resolve is
important. **Indecisive business owners don't succeed.** Keep at it.
You will not succeed without drive and determination.

HOW

Passionately commit to success. *Make a <u>written</u> pledge with yourself to succeed.*
Keep it safe and bring it out from time to time to motivate yourself.

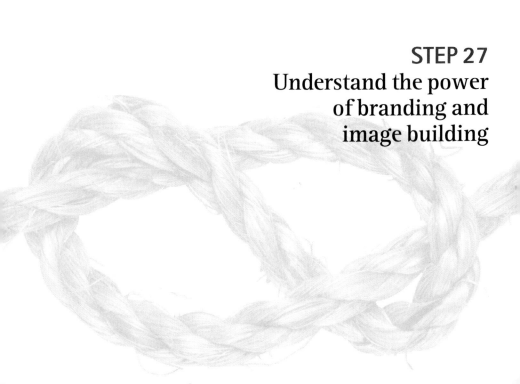

STEP 27
Understand the power of branding and image building

WHY

You have to be different to attract custom. Nowadays in business the choices offered to customers are great. You need loyal customers who identify with you. Even in a small business, branding is important. Branding is not just for Coca Cola! *Don't miss out on this one.*

HOW

Use professionals to design your image. Base your image around customer 'wants'. I know it's obvious, but make sure your business looks the way your selected customers want it to look. Be consistent in the message.

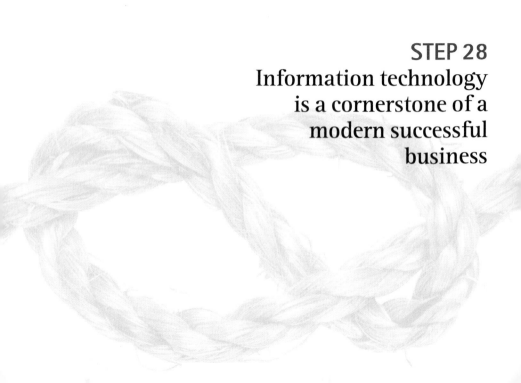

STEP 28
Information technology is a cornerstone of a modern successful business

WHY

Processes form the foundation of any leverage -based business. What better solution to efficient processes than computers? To compete with others you must be hyper-efficient. Commit to information technology to achieve this.

HOW

Invest whatever you can in IT. Become aware of what this means. Make a point of having some understanding of PCs. This gives you perspective. But don't become an IT nerd. Use quality proven software like Microsoft and Sage products.

Don't reinvent the wheel. These companies will have everything you want and more. Just commit strategically to IT as a key tool.

WHY

Just because you own a business it doesn't mean you know it all.

Learning is exciting in itself. You can learn in days from other people's books and tapes knowledge that took them years to gain. This cannot fail to benefit you and your business.

HOW

Buy technical, motivational and self-development books, audio cassettes, videos and CDs. Listen to cassettes to make your car's entertainment system a 'bastion of learning'. Openly share ideas with others. Become a voracious learner. It really is quite infectious once you start.

TO DO'S

"It is impossible to enjoy idling thoroughly unless one has plenty of work to do"

Jerome K Jerome

Steps

STEP 30
Listen to your customers. They will tell you everything you need to know about your business

WHY

In the modern business world, only those businesses that provide the market place and their customers with what they want, will survive and flourish. This applies even to small businesses! You must keep your customers. You must add new customers. You must exceed customers' expectations. Meeting expectations is not good enough any more. This is tough but it is true.

The only way to know what customers want is to talk to them and listen to what they say. *Listening is more important than talking.*

HOW

Hold customer forums. Build long term relationships with your customers. Let customers know how important they are. Live, eat and breathe a customer-led culture. A customer-led culture is going **way** beyond customer service.

STEP 31
Complaining customers who get satisfactorily dealt with can become the best ambassadors for your business

WHY

Odd this. But very true. Everyone knows that things go wrong. No one likes it, but we all experience it. How we deal with problems becomes the true measure of a business. When you satisfactorily deal with a customer, he or she will become your best ambassador. **This point is often missed because businesses become too inward looking.**

HOW

Create a system for customer complaints that is watertight, and I mean watertight. *Monitor it personally and I mean personally.*

STEP 32

Your attitude and demeanour when you enter your business in the morning will dramatically impact how your team of staff feel and act during the day

WHY

More responsibility for you. It's tough at the top! Sometimes we may misuse our power to act in a way we would not tolerate from our team. You must understand the impact this has on others and how it will adversely affect your business and thus you. *This is the true stuff of leadership.*

HOW

If you are not feeling great when you arrive in the car park, take some deep breaths and prepare yourself for your entry. If possible play some motivational tapes on the way to work. *Anything to give yourself a great entrance.* It will, over time, make a real difference.

STEP 33
Surround yourself with positive-thinking and like-minded people

Urgent!

WHY

Sometimes it's not easy being a business owner. It can also be very lonely. Having like-minded, positive people around you can be very supportive. *All evidence shows that mentor groups work.*

HOW

Actively build your positive group. Other positive-thinking successful business owners are perfect. But remember, you must be able to trust their confidentiality and discretion.

STEP 34
Give great loyalty to your team and you will be rewarded with massive commitment

WHY

Some people will let you down. Any team will include difficult and non-committed people. But most people are not like this.

Therefore, set yourself up for success, *by encouraging the majority not the minority.*

HOW

Don't let odd bad experiences distort your beliefs. Focus on the good.
Which set of circumstances do you want to be true?

STEP 35
Choose your advisers well

WHY

Your most important adviser is your accountant or business coach. I would say that, wouldn't I? You cannot know everything yourself. Why not pick others' brains and speed up the process of learning? Advisers who deal with many businesses will gain a broad breadth of understanding and knowledge. Use this to help you.

HOW

Choose advisers with experience. Choose advisers you trust and whose company you enjoy. Choose like-minded advisers. *It is very unwise to change advisers many times in your business life.*

STEP 36
Give great passion to your business (and your life!)

Urgent!

WHY

Without passion, you are dead. Your competitors may be passionate about their businesses. If they are, and you are not, watch out!

HOW

Just do it. If not get out!

STEP 37
Blaming is a massive negative force in a business

WHY

Do you like being blamed? No? So why would anyone else? Blaming creates a defensive mentality which undermines positive thinking. Before you know where you are, you will be blaming your customers! That leads to one thing only. *Fewer customers.*

HOW

Ban blaming. Write it down as a rule. In my office, we call it 'Bushwhacking' and have 'Bushwhacking is Prohibited' signs all over the office.
Little things like this really do count.

STEP 38
Base your pricing primarily upon premium value items or services

Urgent !

WHY

In a small business you probably have a very small share of your market place. Therefore, you can afford to be selective with your customers. Customers will pay premium prices for high perceived value products or services. In fact, evidence shows they react badly to underpaying for high value.

Highlight premium pricing opportunities for products or services that are perceived as high value by your customers.

HOW

Carefully list and identify premium pricing opportunities for customer perceived high value products or services. You will have at least one if not a number of opportunities. If nothing else in this book makes you profit, this will. *Give this area real attention.*

STEP 39
You know by now
.......it's true
you can do it!

Urgent!

WHY

You know why. If you don't.... **sorry, it's back to step one.**

HOW

Just believe it. Read the steps again and write down <u>at</u> <u>least</u> 5 actions you are going to take to make a difference.

Thank you

for considering my ideas. Good luck with implementing them.

Richard Walters

"Go to your business, I say, pleasure, whilst I go to my pleasure, business"

William Wycherley

ABOUT THE AUTHOR

PO Box 6417

Basingstoke RG22 5XN

Richard Walters is best known as the inventor of the Strategic Planning Toolkit, an IT facilitation tool that is sold extensively under licence and franchises across the UK. He is one of the UK's leading authorities on strategic planning for small and medium businesses. Richard is also the inventor and designer of many other planning tools such as Wealth Tracker. He has spent most of his working life successfully advising small businesses.

He started his own small business in 1980 and now operates Harris Walters, a multi-million pound business advisory and accountancy business with a number of partners and offices throughout Hampshire and Wiltshire.

Twenty-five years of helping small businesses of all sizes and all different trades has given Richard a unique perspective on the problems consistently encountered by budding entrepreneurs. Richard is Senior Partner of Harris Walters, Managing Director of Harris Walters Limited and non-executive Finance Director of three other companies, including two manufacturing companies.

He is married with three children, and lives in Hampshire.

For further information regarding the Strategic Planning Toolkit, Wealth Tracker and other products, please visit us on line at www.harriswalters.co.uk

To order other
titles in the
Discover series

ORDER FORM

Please send me copy/copies of: *(please indicate in the space provided)*

_____ Discover the perfect Managing Director of your business: YOU!

_____ Discover the most obvious key to success for your small business: Sales and Marketing

_____ Discover the little gem for your business success: IT!

_____ Discover the perfect successful business for the future: your own Accountancy Practice

_____ Discover the fun of business in your own Legal Practice

Name _____ Position _____

Company _____

Address _____

_____

Telephone _____ Telex/Fax _____

VAT No. (EC companies)_____ Your Order Ref _____

Management Pocketbooks Ltd., 14 East Street, Alresford, Hampshire SO24 9EE
Tel: (01962) 735573 Fax: (01962) 733637 E-mail:pocketbks@aol.com
Web: www.pocketbook.co.uk

The Management Pocketbook Series